Silver:
Past, Present and Your Future

John Michael Weir

ISBN: 9798740471617

DEDICATION

This book is dedicated to all who I have talked finances with and those who have dedicated their lives to education. Even though there are too many to name individually I have gained wisdom and knowledge from each one of you. Two things stand out in my mind, to love what you do and learn something new each day. Thank you for helping ordinary people make better plans for their financial futures.

Contents

ACKNOWLEDGMENTS

I must thank the many Silver stackers (collectors) that I have learned from who are actively protecting their financial future.

Herbert Abraham, Wealth Ambassador who is one of the most positive influencers online.

Stansberry Research and Daniela Cambone who introduces us to the finest economists and knowledge workers in finance.

1 What this book is about

We all have basic needs that must be met for health and happiness. Our financial activities really determine to what extent we can experience freedom. Today we are faced with financial actions never seen. Many accounts say that an amount of US Currency printed in the last year equals nearly 40% of all the US Currency printed since its formation. Economists are saying we have no way to measure the inflation that is building. The stock market is showing volatility building and many of those economists are clearly saying buy hard assets to better protect your future.

Precious metals: gold, silver and others provide safeguards against inflation and other currency resets. The limited amounts and widespread use make these metals especially attractive. Many laws and customs have created relationships between these metals in our monetary system.

The two most common precious metals used in place of currency are gold and silver. The metals have been used for thousands of years to buy or trade for the necessities of life.

We are going to look mostly at silver; past, present and how it can help your future. While silver has been called the poor man's gold it really serves us better. The higher value of gold is used for large purchases and silver more appropriately for day-to-day needs. Imagine trying to buy food with gold and not being able to get change back.

2 history of silver

From the beginning, silver and gold have been known as precious metals. Their initial use was as ornaments due to their elegance. They became widely accepted as popular mediums of exchange due to their demand for this reason. As a result of the monetary use, a new market emerged, which gradually became dominant as the economic system progressed. Metal's value in terms of other goods and their relative prices in terms of each other has changed significantly over time. Differences in the absolute and relative output of gold and silver and their changing popularity as luxuries and a means of trade and their movement between countries have contributed to these variations.

Laws and conventions that have established the relationship between the two metals in the monetary system have also played a role. Since gold was contained in nuggets and dust mixed with sand and could be washed with primitive methods, it was possibly used before silver. On the other hand, silver was usually found in ores and could only be extracted by smelting. However, some silver in its natural state was most likely available in prehistoric Mexico, North America, and Egypt. It was also discovered in electrum, a natural gold alloy.

Silver and Gold
Silver may have been as valuable as gold or even more valuable in ancient times and locations due to the comparatively limited availability of the white metal. On the other hand, silver became more abundant and less valuable as mining and smelting progressed. The two metals were well-known in classical times. During a prosperous time in the sixth and fifth

centuries before Christ, Athens operated silver mines at Laurium and distributed a ten-drachma annual dividend to each resident. Silver was mined from Spanish mines and was an important element in Rome's battles with Carthage.

According to William Jacob, the stock of precious metals had declined to less than 135,000,000 by the year 806 A.D., based on a 10-percent decrease every 36 years due to abrasion and export, but that from then until the discovery of America, mining in Europe was revived to such an extent that the stock was possibly held at about that amount.

The mines at Joachimsthal in Bohemia, which opened at the beginning of the thirteenth century, were among the new silver mines. The Joachimsthaler, later abbreviated to thaler and then corrupted to the dollar, was coined here in the sixteenth century as a name for the Spanish "pieces of eight" and their descendants, which have circulated in so many countries around the world. A declining price level followed the decreasing availability of precious metals during Rome's fall to America's discovery. Even the smallest gold and silver coins were too large for everyday transactions in such conditions.

The Feudal Era
During the feudal era, Europe was largely a barter economy with little currency use. Since an ounce of gold was worth just eight to nine ounces of silver in Asia versus ten to thirteen ounces in Europe, there was a desire to export silver rather than gold in trade with the Orient. In certain ways, gold entered Europe as silver left. On the other hand, the Crusaders occasionally returned with both precious metals as booty.

America's discovery resulted in vast quantities of gold and silver being available. These were initially obtained by Indian plunder. The Spaniards continued to mine extensively after that, especially in Bolivia, Peru, Colombia, and Mexico. At the same time, European mine production was growing. As a result, the overall money supply in Europe increased dramatically.

The introduction of such a large amount of gold and silver into Europe's monetary system ushered in the shift from a swap to a money economy. This process was followed by increasing prices and increased economic growth, all of which had implications on European civilization. Partly through new coinage in various European countries and partly through crude "bits of eight" or coins of eight reads struck in Mexico and South America, American silver entered circulation.

Later, the coin's minting was improved, and it was dubbed the Spanish dollar.

On the obverse, it featured the reigning king's head, and on the reverse, the Spanish arms with the Pillars of Hercules.

The Spanish dollar was kept very close to its original weight and fineness for three centuries, during which time many European coins were debased. As a result, it became a world currency virtually. It was a legal tender in the United States until 1857, and it served as the main means of trade in many Asian countries for a long time. AFTER THE SPANISH AMERICAN COLONIES ' INDEPENDENCE HALTED THEIR COINAGE, Carolus IV's dollars continued to be sought after in China. They gained a scarcity value much greater than their bullion content.

Silver in The Twentieth Century

Long into the twentieth century, there were a few specimens in circulation in China's interior. After Mexico gained independence in 1821, the new government continued to issue the same weight and fineness dollars or pesos with a Mexican republican device until 1904, when the country adopted the gold standard. In the Far East trade, these dollars eventually replaced Spanish dollars.

They accounted for most silver coins in China before the Chinese government started mass-producing silver coins in 1914. In China, the words "Mexican" and "Mex." are still used to differentiate the Chinese dollar from the American or "gold" dollar.

Silver in European History

In the history of European coinage during the sixteenth, seventeenth, and eighteenth centuries, two distinct characteristics stand out. For coinage purposes, the first attempt was to define a fixed value ratio between the two metals. Since different coinage ratios were set in different countries, and because the commercial demand ratio could be different, the coins of whichever metal was undervalued in the coinage ratio were always culled out and exported or melted for sale.

When gold is undervalued, the circulation is dominated by overvalued silver; to remedy this, the government may set a new ratio, but it will almost certainly go too far, causing the reverse process to occur. The English guinea, for example, was priced at 20 shillings silver in 1663 because it was to be coined from gold brought from Guinea in West Africa. Later circumstances caused it to be worth up to 30 shillings, but only in terms of short-weight coins. It was officially set to 22 shillings toward the end of the century and then to 21 shillings in 1717.

While a new 20-shilling sovereign later replaced the guinea coin, the name lives on as a money of account, or rather, as money with which to state professional and club fees, marine insurance rates on heavy risks, and any transactions that are deemed a little superior to the plebeian pounds, shillings, and pence. Another characteristic of the European currency experience was the sovereign power's deliberate debasement of the coinage and the intention to keep it in circulation at its old value. People, in this case, appeared to keep out any undebased coins they had and circulate the overvalued coins as soon as they knew what was going on.

Coinage Ratio

The imperfect adjustment of the coinage ratio to the market ratio, as well as the debasement of the coinage, all explained Sir Thomas Gresham's well-known rule that when two kinds of money have the same nominal value in circulation, the poorer money will push the better money out of circulation because it will be more lucrative for holders of the better money to dispose of it elsewhere. Both metals were commonly used as currency by the nineteenth century's turn. Coin debasement was no longer as popular as it once was. Honesty had proven to be the best strategy after a long and painful experience.

However, the issue of how to set the coinage ratio between the two metals persisted, and it has remained a key question for the next century and a third. It has disappeared for long periods before reappearing. The story of silver money is the story of numerous attempts to solve it. History of Silver For the two decades between 1851 and 1870, global gold output was nearly equal to that of the previous three and a half centuries. In less than a decade, the world's gold supply was effectively doubled. However, there was no substantial rise in silver prices. From 1493 to 1850, total silver production was approximately 33 times that of gold in terms of weight and more than twice that of gold in terms of value. For the next two decades, silver production was less than six times that of gold in terms of weight. By 1870, the total amount of silver produced since 1493 had only been around 20 times that of gold in terms of weight, or li times in terms of value.

Influx of Silver

Furthermore, the vast influx of silver to the Far East had most likely left a monetary stock in the West that was at least half gold in value. Before

1850, silver was unquestionably the more important monetary metal. However, by 1870, enough gold was available in the Western world to make the gold standard a viable option. This possibility became a reality in all major financial countries over the next decade. Since 1816, England has been legally bound by the gold standard. In 1854, Portugal took advantage of fresh gold supplies to join the gold standard.

The rest of Europe was on silver or bimetallic standards in 1870, but there was widespread support for gold. Numerous papers were written on the merits of a standardized gold standard and a uniform international coinage, though some favored bimetallism's continuation. The French government was a firm supporter of the gold standard and had not been for the Franco-Prussian War of 1870-1871, and the Latin Monetary Union would have adopted it. Because of the Franco-Prussian War, Germany was different from her adversary, allowing her to foresee France's adoption of the gold standard.

Before the war, the German states worked on a silver standard, with a limited amount of gold in circulation at market value rather than a set ratio. Late in 1871, with the French indemnity of five billion francs (approximately $1,000,000,000) in hand, the emerging German Empire took the first step toward a gold standard. A law was made that allowed for the minting of new gold coins at a coinage ratio of 15.5 to 1 about existing silver coins and the suspension of the production of any additional large silver coins. The mark was to be the unit, which was equal to 5.531 grains of fine gold.

1873 Legislation

Another legislation, passed in July 1873, formally created the gold standard and authorized the minting of new silver coins with a one-tenth reduction in weight from the current standard, resulting in a coinage ratio of 13.95 to 1 as opposed to 14.95 to 1 for American and 14.38 to 1 for Latin Monetary Union subsidiary coins. Of course, these coins were only to be minted for government use. They were to be legal tender up to the value of 20 marks, with a total issue limit of 20 marks per capita. Old silver coins were to be phased out of circulation, but they maintained full legal tender rights until they were phased out.

More than 1,000,000,000 marks of old silver coins were removed under this initiative, with more than a third being recoined. Most of the remainder, 7,104,800 metric pounds (of 500 grams), or approximately 114,000,000 fine ounces, was sold between 1873 and 1879, with most sales occurring after 1875. Around 450,000,000 marks of the old thaler coins were still in circulation, with full legal tender force. Regardless of when actual sales occurred, the passage of the first legislation in December 1871 served as a direct warning to the world's silver industry.

With a price ratio of about 15.5 to 1, fewer than 400,000 francs of silver 5-franc pieces were minted in France in 1872. Nearly 155,000,000 francs in silver were proposed for coinage in 1873. In Belgium, a similar situation occurred. If the ratio continues to increase above 15.5 to 1, the Latin Monetary Union's gold currency would be quickly replaced by silver, just as it did in the 1850s. As a result, the Union's countries were forced to take a series of measures to shield themselves from the substitution of gold with silver. In November 1873, France and Belgium put a regular limit on the amount of silver that could be coined. Belgium passed legislation in December allowing the government to suspend the production of 5-franc coins. At the request of Switzerland, a Union conference convened in Paris in January 1874.

Belgium and Switzerland called for a gold standard at the conference, while France and Italy preferred to maintain the status quo, with certain restrictions on the amount of silver coinage. The latter proposal won out, and in 1874, it was agreed to restrict the coinage of 5-franc pieces to 60,000,000 francs in France and smaller quantities in the rest of the world, for a total of 120,000,000 francs. The agreement made no mention of limiting the public's ability to present silver for free coinage within the defined limits.

Free Coinage

France continued to allow free coinage based on "first-come, first-served." On the other hand, the other three nations refused to coin individuals. Instead, they bought silver at market price for coinage, resulting in a seigniorage benefit of 15.5 to 1 over the market ratio. In 1875 and 1876, the restrictions were maintained, and in the latter year, France stripped away individuals' right to free coinage.

Finally, the Union suspended the coinage of 5-franc pieces in 1878, except that Italy could coin a small amount to enable the return to specie payments after a long period of the depreciated paper. The depreciation of silver prompted other European countries to abandon the gold standard. In 1873, Denmark and Sweden, later joined by Norway, established the Scandinavian Monetary Union, which placed all these countries' currencies on a gold standard, replacing previous silver standards.

They sold some silver, but it was small compared to Germany's huge sales. From 1816 to 1847, Holland used a bimetallic standard and then switched to a silver standard. The Bank of the Netherlands ended a twenty-year tradition of purchasing all silver sold at a fixed rate in 1872, and the government began minting silver coins in 1873.

Another law passed in 1875 allowed for the continued suspension of silver coinage and the coining of gold at a ratio of 15.625 to 1. After 1873, the silver coins gained a scarcity value. A law was passed in 1883 authorizing the melting and selling of 25,000,000 florins of silver coins, but it was only used to provide silver for subsidiary coinage. In 1876, Russia halted the production of silver coins for individuals, except silver needed for trade with China. Spain stopped issuing silver coins to individuals in 1878, but it persisted on a government account. In 1879, Austria-Hungary stopped issuing free silver coins. There were no mints in Europe by 1880 where silver could be presented for free coinage.

There was still some demand for silver for government-issued subsidiary coins, but these were only of small legal tender. Simultaneously, large silver coins were issued under previous laws in many nations, retaining their maximum legal-tender qualities and serving as a significant circulation and bank reserve component. Most European countries could not be said to be entirely on the gold standard because of the presence of these legal-tender silver coins, but they were on the limping standard. Some people used depreciated paper from time to time, but no one went back to free silver coinage. In India and China, the white metal was still used, but gold was to become Western countries' currency.

3 The fall in the price of silver

The price of silver had shown a downward trend, with fluctuations, during the decade from 1870 to 1880. It reached a spectacular low of 46f pence per ounce, or a ratio of 20.17 to 1, in July 1876, but for most of the decade, it was between $1.10 (or 50 pence) $1.20 (or 55 pence) per ounce. The price continued in a downward direction until 1893. The reasons for this great fall in price, extending over twenty years, have been a subject of considerable controversy, partly because of the complexity of the economic forces operating and partly because contemporary discussion lacked the necessary perspective.

The following were probably among the most important factors:

A fundamental cause was that, whereas before 1850, silver and gold both had been important monetary metals, the great gold production of the next two decades supplied enough gold to take the place of silver in large measure. The great advantage of gold as a standard for large transactions made it preferable, and, as we have seen, Europe generally adopted it in the 1870s.

Thus, the monetary demand for silver in the Western world was largely removed, leaving only Asia's. This naturally tended to make the price fall since there were no longer any mints to receive silver at a fixed price.

Adoption of Gold Standard

The adoption of the gold standard in a way overshot its mark. The production of gold fell off in the 1870s and 1880s, and at the same time, world industry and commerce were expanding. The supply of gold was hardly adequate for the world's needs. From about 1865 to 1896, there was a long period of falling commodity prices ascribed by many to the shortage of gold. Since the price of silver no longer was pegged by free coinage, it declined other commodity prices.

At the same time, the production of silver was increasing, in large part because of the exploitation of the Comstock lode in Nevada. The average annual world production rose from about 25,000,000 ounces in the 1840s to about 40,000,000 in the 1860s, 70,000,000 in the 1870s, 100,000,000 in the 1880s, and 160,000,000 in the 1890s.

This rapid increase tended to lower the price. These three forces certainly were sufficient, when taken together, to account for the general downward trend. The minor, or sometimes violent, fluctuations in the price are explained by more temporary causes, by the psychology of the market as influenced by the twenty-year discussion of the silver question, and by the varying national and international actions taken. The fall of silver caused some reconsideration of demonetization.

4 The importance of silver

Silver remains a critical product for both manufacturing and investment purposes today. Many investors, however, want to know more about what makes silver such a valuable commodity.

Let us look at some of the key reasons why silver is so important before going into the history of the phenomenon:

In the earth's crust, there is a relative lack of resources. A wide range of industrial uses.

There is a fundamental appeal that transcends time and space.

We have a detailed understanding of why silver remains important after decades in the precious metals industry and countless hours of study. The following sections will go over these explanations in greater depth.

The origins of gold and silver's use as currency, like any subject buried beneath the sands of time, elicit some debate among historians, as well as anthropologists, archaeologists, and academia at large.

Competing scholars on this topic present small variations in their work when providing the same overall narrative. Settlement of exchange and trade in precious metals proved to be a more effective method than mere barter throughout the ancient world.

Some scholars disagree on when and where this practice began and whether it spread across the inhabited world or originated independently in multiple cultures, such as silver for trade in India, before contacting Greece.

In any case, by the time of documented history in antiquity, nearly all Central Asia's tribes or cultures were doing business with gold and silver ingots.

Use of Precious Metals as Money

Precious metals are great for use as money for a variety of purposes. Suppose it is possible that these elements were put to the same use by various cultures long ago in humanity's history by chance. In that case, it is also possible that we will discover that the ancients understood more than we think.

The theory that ancient peoples chose gold and silver as money deliberately (rather than a result of a random historical circumstance) is based on modern science and industry lessons.

Through thousands of years of exploration (and plenty of trial-and-error), gold and silver have been discovered to be more than just shiny metals. True, their distinctive colors and luster are not insignificant, but there is a reason these metals have always been referred to as "precious."

The name is not selected at random: Silver and gold have unique properties that make them extremely useful to humans.

Approximately half of the silver mined is used in industrial processes every year. This contrasts with gold, which has significant industrial uses but is only used in limited quantities. Industry consumes less than ten percent of freshly mined gold per year.

Silver has a wide range of applications, including most electronics. Silver, for example, is what makes your smartphone screen work. Silver is commonly used to cover medical equipment. Silver is present in solar panels' photovoltaic cells.

Silver is used in several traditional industries. It helps to give mirrors their reflective surface by coating them. Silver has been used in photography for a long time. Silver is used in many long-life batteries and being used in many devices.

These are merely a few examples, but they all have something to do with precious metals' chemistry and physics. On the Periodic Table of Elements, silver's chemical symbol is Ag. This is derived from the Latin word Argentum, which means "silver." It is still referred to as the "argent alloy" on occasion.

Silver, while being mostly non-reactive with other compounds, can be an excellent catalyst in many chemical reactions. Silver's high malleability allows it to easily take on various shapes, which is significant in producing jewelry and other products like cutlery. Consider this: we commonly refer to all eating utensils as "silverware," a term that refers to this historical usage.

Silver Properties

Silver is also ductile, which ensures it can be twisted into thin wires. Furthermore, it is the most effective metal for conducting electricity and one of the strongest heat conductors.

The color of silver is the most noticeable physical property that comes to mind. Owing to their identical appearance, it is often grouped with platinum and palladium as "white metals." Nonetheless, silver's lustrous color is unmistakable and well-known in the world.

It is a relatively dense metal but not as dense as palladium, gold, or platinum (in order of density). In addition to being malleable, silver has a melting point in the middle of the pack compared to other elements, reaching a liquid state at 962 degrees Celsius (roughly 1,764 degrees Fahrenheit).

These qualities, when combined, have made silver a valuable metal for purposes other than industrial use.

The most obvious example is how silver (along with gold) has often lent itself to being used as currency.

Silver is among the few items that have been accessible to humanity since the dawn of time. As previously mentioned, the use of silver as a means of currency by ancient peoples is unlikely to be a coincidence. It just so happens that many of silver's chemical and physical properties make it an excellent money metal.

Here are some of silver's most significant monetary characteristics:

- Unlike many barter products, silver can be divided into small units of equal composition.

- Silver prevents corrosion and is long-lasting, allowing it to circulate for longer periods. It's a non-perishable commodity.
- Silver can be conveniently transported over long distances without decaying, related to the first two qualities.
- Silver's recognizability implies that it is easily recognized as having value, making it a successful trade medium regardless of place.
- Silver has a long history of retaining its buying power compared to other products, services, and resources over thousands of years.
- Given these characteristics, it's no surprise that the word "money" is synonymous with, or derived directly from, the word "silver" in at least a dozen languages.
- Silver's strong connection to wealth has resulted from its possession of these characteristics. The elite of most cultures has continued to use silver for ceremonial objects that are usually made of less costly metals.

This connection can be traced back to the beginning of human history. Silver was more precious than gold in Ancient Egypt's early days because it was scarcer than gold. Silver was thought to be a divine material by the Egyptians, as the bones of gods were said to be made of it.

For the same cause, merchants and traders worldwide were enamored with silver coins. For centuries, silver was one of the few types of money that could be trusted while transacting business.

Silver coins, for example, were the predominant means of exchange in the Middle East and North Africa well into the nineteenth century. The Maria Theresa thaler, a silver trade coin issued by the Habsburg Empire based in Austria-Hungary, was particularly common among Arab merchants. (In German, the word "thaler" means "dollar.")

Silver's lustrous luster and tangible existence (as opposed to "paper assets") are also considered wealth indicators. Over the years, many high-net-worth individuals and royalty members have favored silver—something tangible and tangible—to more abstract financial instruments.

Western Countries on Silver Trade

As a result, several Western countries released their silver trade dollars for use in the East. During the 1800s and into the early years of the 1900s, large silver coins were shipped to China. In North America, the Spanish silver dollar (or eight reales) was widely used in commerce and was embraced as legal tender in the United States until after the Civil War.

There are numerous examples of silver's former position in global trade. During the British Empire's dominance, Britain's currency, the pound sterling, was named to rely on sterling silver (92.5 percent pure silver).

During World War I, the British council agreed to pay its colonial subjects in India in silver for their services. Since silver (or gold, which was in short supply) was the only type recognized by the Indians, it received 270 million silver dollars from the United States.

These are very small examples of how, until recently, silver's recognizability made it the ideal currency for foreign trade and debt settlement.

Silver coins have all but vanished as currency in the last half-century. In 1965, the United States began producing 90% silver coins for daily circulation, and nearly the entire world followed suit.

Silver is now traded in the same way as any other asset. Most of its price is dictated by supply and demand. Jewelry, manufacturing applications, and investment purposes make up nearly equal parts of its demand profile.

On the investment side, bullion coins issued by various government mints for the express purpose of investment and trade are now joining silver bars.

Per year, more than 30,000 metric tons of silver are extracted. Surprisingly, primary silver mines account for just a small portion of this total. Instead, most of the newly extracted silver is produced as a by-product of other mining activities, such as copper, gold, and zinc mines, where silver occurs naturally in the same ore as these other metals.

As a result, the silver mining industry has seen many restructurings, with many firms merging to achieve more efficiencies. This can also lower each mine's all-in sustaining cost (AISC), the cost of service per ounce of silver mined.

Traditional "safe havens" provide several asset classes with relatively stable values during periods of market stress. Government bonds (especially U.S. Treasury bonds), gold, and certain reserve currencies are the most popular safe havens.

Safe-haven assets add to a portfolio's diversification. This means that having a diverse portfolio of assets whose individual output is not highly correlated reduces overall risk. It is one of the attributes that gold and silver have in common, contributing to their investment appeal.

Silver coins, like the American Silver Eagle, will offer even more diversification, balance, and security to anyone who already owns gold.

As compared to other precious metals, the price of silver has a very low entry point. As a result, it will appeal to any investor, regardless of their financial situation. Furthermore, holding a mix of gold and silver in your portfolio ensures that you will not be left out if one of the metals outperforms the other.

To be honest, the demand for safe-haven investments is increasing. This is because of a variety of factors. As a nearly decade-long bull market comes to an end, the global economy is entering a time of transition. Not only is this cycle coming to an end, forcing some investors to take on more risk in search of dwindling returns, but what lies ahead is truly unknown territory.

Aftermath of 2008 Financial Crisis
Following the financial crisis of 2008, policymakers took unprecedented measures. Markets have stabilized thanks to large amounts of economic stimulus, but the unwinding of these extreme policies has created new obstacles that are difficult to foresee.

This collection of circumstances makes it much more important for investors to use an appropriate hedge to protect themselves. The argument for silver's value as an investment is supported by both the long-term historical context and current market conditions' vagaries.

Without question, silver has continued to appreciate at a price over time, preserving its value against inflation. Due to this, many in the financial industry refer to it as an "inflation hedge."

What is the significance of this? That the world's currencies behave in a completely different way. Inflation is a relative loss of value for a currency as prices for goods and services rise. The mechanism is intensified by the rise in the money supply over time: When more currency enters the economy, each unit appears to buy less than it did previously.

A stamp is perhaps the best example of this. For a long time, a stamp in the United States cost 3 cents. You could get 33 stamps for a dollar (with a penny to spare). Even though nothing about stamps has changed, stamp prices have gradually risen.

What is the current price of a traditional stamp? More than 50 is the solution. You cannot even get two of them for a dollar. When seen through the prism of inflation, it is easier to believe that money's buying power has decreased rather than that a stamp's "value" has risen.

This is not exclusive to the U.S. dollar. Inflation wreaks havoc on fiat currencies in general. "Paper money finally returns to its intrinsic value—zero," wrote the famous French philosopher Voltaire.

With all of this in mind, silver's worth is about maintaining buying power. Its appeal is more akin to a form of investment than a speculative venture in the long run.

Another advantage of silver is its high liquidity. Liquidity refers to how quickly and efficiently anything can be sold without having a major price change. This is especially useful in the case of a "rainy day" or an emergency since it will help you remain afloat even if the economy is down, or your life is interrupted suddenly.

Of course, no one can foresee the future, but silver is a low-risk investment for any investor.

5 Other uses for silver

Silver, the white metal, has a storied tradition of use in jewelry and coins, but it is still mainly used in industry. New technologies are continually emerging to take advantage of silver's unique properties, whether in mobile phones or solar panels.

Silver is a rare and valuable precious metal, and it is a noble metal that prevents corrosion and oxidation, but not as well as gold. Silver is suitable for electrical applications since it is the greatest thermal and electrical conductor among all metals. It can be used in medicine and consumer goods because of its antimicrobial and non-toxic properties. It is ideal for jewelry, silverware, and mirrors because of its high luster and reflectivity. Its malleability enables it to be flattened into sheets. Its flexibility allows it to be drawn into thin, flexible wire, making it the ideal option for various industrial applications. In the meantime, its photosensitivity has earned it a place in the world of film photography.

Silver's Cost

Silver is much less costly than gold since it is more plentiful. Silver may be powdered, pasted, shaved into flakes, reduced to a salt, alloyed with other metals, flattened into printable sheets, drawn into wires, suspended as a colloid, or even used as a catalyst. Silver's long history of coinage and jewelry ensures that it will continue to shine in the manufacturing arena. However, its reputation as a sign of wealth and prestige will be preserved. The most common use of silver in the industry is in electronics. Since silver has the best thermal and electrical conductivity of any metal, it cannot be easily substituted by less costly materials.

Tiny amounts of silver, for example, are used as contacts in electrical switches: connect the contacts, and the switch turns on; separate the contacts, and the switch turns off. Using a traditional switch to turn on a bedroom light or a membrane switch to turn on a microwave, the result is the same: current can only move through when the contacts are joined. Market products, like automobiles, have a plethora of contacts that monitor electronic functions. Silver is also used in industrial switches.

Where does silver come from, and how does it get to these electronic devices? Silver is extracted from silver mines or a by-product of lead and zinc mines. Silver is extracted from the ore by smelting and refining. The silver is then usually shaped into bars or grains. Silver of the highest purity is required for electronic applications: 99.99 percent pure, also known as the fineness of 999.9.

As pure silver is dissolved in nitric acid, silver nitrate is formed, powdered, or flaked. This material can then be fabricated into contacts or silver pastes, such as silver-palladium alloy conductive paste.

Silver paste has several applications, including the membrane switch described earlier and the rear defrosts in many automobiles. Silver paste is used in electronics to make circuit paths and passive components such as multilayer ceramic capacitors (MLCCs). Photovoltaic cells for solar energy production are among the fastest-growing uses of silver paste.

Nano silver, or silver with incredibly small particle sizes (1-100 nanometers, or 1-100 billionths of a meter), opens up a new frontier for technical advancement because it needs much less silver to accomplish the same task. Nano silver conductive inks are used in printed electronics. The electrode present in the supercapacitor, which can charge and discharge repeatedly and rapidly, is an example of a printed electronic. Regenerative braking is an automotive invention that stores a slowing vehicle's kinetic energy in a supercapacitor for later use. Another useful use of printed electronics is radio frequency identification (RFID) tags. These tags are superior to bar codes for product monitoring because they store more data and can be read from farther away, even without a clear line of sight.

Silver can also be used in consumer electronics. If your plasma television set has a silver electrode to enhance image quality, it can use silver for more than merely the on-off switch. Silver electrodes are also used in light-emitting diodes (LEDs) to generate low-level, energy-efficient light. In the meantime, the DVDs and C.D.s you use are likely to have a thin silver recording sheet.

Silver's Uses

Silver oxide or silver zinc alloy batteries are another electronic use of silver. This high-capacity, light-weight batteries outperform other batteries at high temperatures. Silver-oxide is used in camera and watch button batteries and aerospace and defense applications. For laptop computers and electric vehicles, silver-zinc batteries are a viable alternative to lithium batteries.

Superconductors are at the cutting edge of technology. Silver is not a superconductor; when combined with one, it can transmit electricity faster than the superconductor alone. Superconductors bear electricity with little to no resistance at extremely low temperatures. They can produce magnetic energy for driving magnetic levitation trains or turning motors.

The numerous applications of silver in electronics provide an eye-opening look at how one of history's most popular metals has evolved into a cutting-edge future material. Silver is often preferred over other, less costly materials due to its special property with the highest thermal and electrical conductivity.

Solar panels are made with silver paste, as previously mentioned. Photovoltaic cells with silver paste contacts absorb and hold electrical current. When the sun's energy strikes the cell's semiconducting layer, this current is produced. One of the fastest-growing applications for silver is photovoltaic cells.

Silver's reflectivity allows it to play an additional role in solar energy. It reflects solar energy into collectors that produce electricity using salts.

Silver is also used in nuclear power. The white metal is commonly used in control rods in nuclear reactors to absorb neutrons and slow the fission rate. The reaction is slowed when the control rods are inserted into the nuclear core, but it is sped up when they are removed.

Silver's high tensile strength and ductility are used in brazing and soldering to build joints between two metal parts. Temperatures above 600°C are used for brazing, while temperatures below 600°C are used for soldering. Since these processes do not require very pure metal, silver scrap may be used in brazing and soldering. From heating and air conditioning vents to brazing, plumbing and soldering create tight joints. The antibacterial properties of silver and its non-toxicity to humans make it an excellent substitute for lead-based water pipe connections.

Ethylene oxide and formaldehyde are two essential chemicals generated using silver as a catalyst. Molded plastics, such as plastic handles, and flexible plastics, such as polyester, are manufactured from ethylene oxide. It is also a key component of antifreeze. Formaldehyde is a chemical used to produce solid plastics, resins, and protective coatings. It is also used as an antiseptic and embalming fluid. Silver acts as a catalyst, speeding up reactions without being consumed.

Some common uses of silver include jewelry and silverware. Silver is a lovely choice because of its malleability, reflectivity, and luster. Silver must be alloyed with different base metals like copper because it is so delicate, as in sterling silver (92.5 percent silver, 7.5 percent copper). Silver can tarnish, despite its resistance to oxidation and corrosion, but it can shine for a lifetime with a little polish. Silver is a common choice for jewelry and a fine dining standard because it is less costly than gold. Base metals with silver plating are a less expensive alternative to silver. Silverware can be accompanied by silver dishes and bowls, which are also ornately made works of art. For example, Paul Revere (1734-1818), best known for his midnight ride at the beginning of the American Revolution, was a silversmith, and the Boston Museum of Fine Arts still has some of his work on display.

Before the recent emergence of digital media, photography was one of the most popular industrial uses of silver. The light sensitivity of silver halide crystals in the film is used in conventional film photography. As the silver halide crystals in the film are exposed to light, they shift and record a latent image transformed into a photograph. This method is useful for non-digital consumer imaging, video, and X-rays because of its precision.

The "silver screen" of cinema should not be confused with the silver used in film photography. This term refers to the silver lenticular screen on which early films were projected, rather than the silver in the film itself.

By consuming oxygen, silver ions serve as a catalyst, killing bacteria by interfering with their respiration. Silver has played an important role in medicine for thousands of years due to its antibiotic properties and lack of toxicity. Silver foil was wrapped around wounds to boost their heal, and colloidal silver and silver-protein complexes were swallowed or applied topically to combat illness before antibiotics were widely used. Silver has also been used to avoid infection in eye drops and dental hygiene.

Although silver is not poisonous, it can cause argyria if consumed in small quantities over time. When people with this disorder are exposed to light, silver builds up in their body tissue, giving it a grey-blue color. Furthermore, ingesting significant quantities of silver may have negative health implications. For these reasons, medical doctors advise against using colloidal silver, despite arguments from some that it is a miracle dietary supplement.

Antibiotic-resistant superbugs are rising the market for silver in hospitals today. To avoid the spread of bacteria, small quantities of silver may be applied to hospital surfaces and medical equipment. Silver prevents wounds from infection when used in medical instruments, wound dressings, and ointments. Silver sulfadiazine is particularly beneficial to burn victims because it destroys bacteria while allowing the skin to regenerate. Silver ion treatments can help cure bone infections and enable damaged tissue to regenerate.

Silver is almost entirely translucent when polished. Mirrors have been created by coating a clear glass surface with a thin layer of silver since the 19th century, while modern mirrors often use other metals such as aluminum. Many new buildings have a translucent coating of silver on their windows that reflects sunlight and keeps the interior cool in the summer. Silver-coated tiles shield satellites from the sun in the aerospace industry.

Silver is used in engine bearings. The most robust bearing is made of steel that has been silver electroplated. Because of its high melting point, silver can withstand the high temperatures used in engines. Silver also serves as a lubricant between a ball bearing and its housing, reducing friction. Silver is being investigated as a potential replacement for platinum in catalyzing the oxidation of matter stored in diesel engine filters due to its ability to absorb oxygen.

Silver's Use as Awards

Silver is used to award second place due to its position as a precious metal that ranks second only to gold. The Olympic Silver Medal for second place is the most well-known silver prize. Many military organizations, employers, clubs, and societies use silver or silver-colored certificates to recognize individuals for their achievements because silver symbolizes honor, courage, and achievement.

Since silver containers and coins were known to prevent liquid spoilage for thousands of years, long before discovering microbial life, silver's antibacterial properties were used. Silver ions in water purification systems hold oxygen that oxidizes and destroys microbes, and a silver coating avoids bacterial build-up in carbon-based water filters. Silver-copper ions can also sanitize lakes and tanks instead of corrosive chlorine.

Silver's antimicrobial properties, which have long been used in medicine and water purification, are now being used in food and hygiene as well. Food packaging and refrigerators are coated with nano silver. Antibacterial silver is also advertised on many new consumer goods, including washing machines, garments, and personal care products.

There are a variety of other common uses for silver. Silver, for example, is one of the ingredients in the amalgam used to fill dental cavities. Still, due to the prevalence of harmful mercury in amalgam, other products have increasingly replaced it. Instruments such as flutes have also been plated with platinum.

Silver is being used in a variety of new ways. As a wood preservative, silver is one of several choices for replacing toxic chromate copper arsenate. The potential of nano silver inks and coatings on paper to avoid the spread of bacterial infection is touted. Silver metal glass is created by rapidly cooling silver and provides long-lasting strength and resistance to deformation. At room temperature, silver-based ionic liquids, which are in a liquid state, can clean up petroleum waste products. Touch screen users can keep their gloves on in cold weather thanks to the silver in the fabric.

Silver seems to have as many applications as the human imagination allows. Traditional silver works, such as jewelry and silverware, rely on the artist's imagination. Modern uses depend on scientists' and engineers ' inventiveness to meet the changing demands of customers and industries. Although some uses, such as silver in photographic film, rise, and fall, others, such as photovoltaic cells' burgeoning development for solar energy, may continue to expand. Like a one-of-a-kind silver band, silver's unique properties, such as its high thermal and electrical conductivity, reflectivity, and antibacterial properties, make it impossible to replace.

6 Use of silver in coins and investments

Silver, along with gold, has long been the metal of choice for coinage. Silver is a valuable and rare precious metal that can store money. People used to accumulate wealth by investing in silver coins, but now they invest in investment-grade silver bullion. Silver will last for a long time because it does not rust and only melts at a reasonably high temperature, and its high luster makes it appealing. Silver is a popular choice for designing and minting local currency because of its malleability.

Silver has been used as currency more often than gold because it is more plentiful and less costly. Many thousands of years ago, silver was mined and traded, and it was first minted into silver coins in the Mediterranean region hundreds of years ago. Different countries used a silver or gold standard before the twentieth century, backing up their currency's value with the inclusion of gold or silver in the treasury. Today, countries make coins out of less costly metals like copper and nickel, and they use fiat currency, in which the value is determined by government control rather than a gold or silver standard.

Gold, as a commodity, maintains its value. Many people invest in silver by purchasing and holding 99.9% pure silver bullion bars, coins, or medallions or using financial instruments such as stocks and mutual funds. Countries also make silver collector's edition coins, which they sell to customers for more than the silver value of the coin.

7 The combination of silver, copper and gold

Any supporter of a new currency in history must make a critical decision. What would be the basis for the unit of account?

Metal-based currencies have been the most popular. The first explanation is that they are naturally resistant to inflation.

The scarcity of something determines its worth. Since there is only so much gold and silver in circulation and only so much new gold and silver mined each year, gold and silver hold their value. The expense of mining, minting, and selling gold and silver coins means that the demand will never be oversupplied. According to tradition, new gold and silver production has remained surprisingly steady for decades.

Unlike paper money, which can be inflated at the whim of politicians or bankers, precious metals remain scarce despite inflationary efforts.

The tendency of paper currencies is the opposite. Politicians and bankers have been as willing to increase the amount of paper money as the public has been to obtain gold and silver throughout history. In certain situations, the motives are good. Many economists and politicians agree that an "elastic currency" would help meet consumer demands, keep people working, and spur new production.

Increase in U.S. Dollar's Price

Despite their good intentions, precious metals-based currencies have outperformed paper currencies. During the 19th century, the U.S. dollar nearly doubled in value as it was focused on gold. Over the twentieth century, it lost over 90% of its value as a paper currency.

Precious metals-based currencies do not depend solely on the assumption that politicians and bankers would not inflate them, nor on third parties continue to recognize them as units of exchange. Precious metals have intrinsic value as well. Precious metals are prized for their use in jewelry, industry, and technology, in addition to their value as a unit of exchange. Aside from its use as gold, an ounce of silver has value. Print money does not.

Even a currency based on precious metals may serve as a representative or commodity. Paper banknotes are used in symbolic money structures and are redeemable for a fixed quantity of gold, silver, or another hard commodity. As a result, they are slightly less vulnerable to inflation. According to the issuer, each note represents a claim to a limited amount of gold or silver.

Representative capital, on the other hand, is not foolproof. It is still based on trust. Holders of banknotes must trust that the bank will have enough gold or silver on hand to redeem all the notes it has issued. They must also trust policymakers not to allow fractional reserves, which means that bankers can have less gold or silver on hand than is needed to fulfill all of their obligations.

Politicians and bankers have struggled to maintain this confidence not only with metal-based currencies but also with paper. Currently, banks in the United States are only allowed to hold 10% of their total deposits on hand. When you deposit $100 in your savings account, $90 is automatically loaned out at a rate of interest while remaining eligible for withdrawal. It is easy to see how the dollar will lose value under such a scheme.

Commodity currency systems, such as Open Currency, do not rely on third-party confidence in any way. Holders of these complementary currencies still have the coin's intrinsic value in their hands. Regardless of what others think, a tenth-ounce gold or silver coin is the tenth ounce of gold or silver. Merchants who sell their goods for a commodity currency should rest assured that their goods will be valued equally. For future consumption or investment in new output, the value remains unchanged over time.

In a world of bloated paper, a commodity currency system based on precious metals is the best complementary currency.

Silver Coins

Before 1964, the United States Mint produced several silver coins. Silver nickels, dimes, quarters, half dollars, and dollars were among the coins. Between 1986 and 2008, the silver one-ounce American Eagle $1 coin was minted. The half dollar, minted between 1965 and 1970, and the Eisenhower dollar, minted between 1971 and 1976, are two other coins made with 40% silver. You will pay with the face value of your silver coins if you want to use them as money. However, you will get a better deal if you exchange them for their silver or collectible value.

Calculation of your Silver Coins' Worth

Find out how much your silver coins are worth by looking at their face value. Look on the back of each coin to achieve this. If you are having trouble reading the coin's worth, use a magnifying glass. Silver nickels, dimes, quarters, half dollars, dollars, and the silver ounce were all produced by the United States Mint (American Eagle).

Using can CoinNews.net silver calculator to figure out how much silver your coins are worth. "US Silver Coin Melt Calculator" requires you to follow the steps outlined below:

Update the sum in the "spot price" field. After that, choose the kind of silver coin you own. Just fill in the blanks with the number of coins of that sort you have. To find out how much silver your coins are worth, go to the "Calculate" page. If you have several silver coins (nickels, quarters, half dollars, and dollars), repeat these steps to assess their silver worth.

Decide if you want to sell your coins for face value, the silver value measured by CoinNews.net, or collectible value.

Offer your silver coins at any place where you are making a transaction for their face value. The merchant is likely to accept the coins at face value. For example, if you use a $1 silver coin, the vendor will consider it as if it were worth a dollar.

Silver Value of Coins

Instead of using your coins for their face value, think of using them for their silver value. To do so, take your coins to a coin or silver dealer and discuss how much money you can get for their silver material. The CoinNews.net website's U.S. silver coin calculator can offer you an estimate of how much your coins are worth in silver material, so bargain with the coin or silver dealer accordingly.

Your final choice is to discuss your coins' collectible value with a coin or silver dealer. Not all silver coins are collectible, and their physical condition impacts how much they are worth. Silver coins from the late 1800s and early 1900s are widely regarded as collectible. Newer coins with unusual qualities can be collectible as well.

Silver's Importance

Silver is now more precious than gold and will remain so for the rest of time. We will operate solely on current silver output from this point forward, and demand will still outstrip supply. [Can you just imagine what that means for the price of this precious metal in the future? Forget about the famous phrase, "Have you got gold?" 'Got silver?' is a far more relevant – and potentially lucrative – query to pose these days.]

Silver is different from gold in many respects. The most notable difference is that, unlike gold, silver is consumed and then lost forever. Almost all the gold that has ever been found in the history of mankind is still here. Gold is primarily used for currency, as a store of wealth, and for ornamentation, such as jewelry. Silver is used in a variety of fields. Its natural antibiotic properties make it an outstanding medical tool. It is used in military applications and electrical switches, relays, and batteries of all sorts. It is a key component in water purification systems and paints and the photographic industry. Silver is a non-corroding metal of excellent thermal conductivity. For millennia, silver, like gold, has been used, and continues to be used, as a monetary tool. Furthermore, as India and China make unprecedented strides toward entering the developed world's ranks, the situation will worsen.

The plot thickens! As if the drastic rise in global demand was not complicated enough, silver is once again being rediscovered as a viable investment option. Barclay's latest silver Exchange Traded Fund is possibly the most recent and the most notable. Barclay's ETF has recently withdrawn a massive amount of silver from the market.

Mining of Silver

Why can't we just go out and mine some more silver? The cost of extracting more silver is why we cannot "fix" the problem. One ounce of gold, for example, costs $350 to $450 to mine, refine, and bring to market today. This is a profitable venture with gold currently trading about $1800 per ounce. Silver, on the other hand, is mainly mined as a by-product. The cost of mining one ounce of silver as a primary metal is equivalent to the expenditure of mining one ounce of gold, and with silver selling about $25 an ounce, it is not even close to profitable when mining costs are considered. We mine approximately 600 million ounces of silver per year, while the industry consumes approximately 870 million ounces. Do you think there will be a disparity? The business is getting tenser.

The silver to gold ratio has been somehow fifteen to one. One ounce of gold is usually bought with fifteen ounces of silver. With silver currently selling at around $25 per ounce and gold at around $1800 per ounce, one ounce of gold requires 65 ounces of silver. This indicates a clear opportunity, as once this ratio reverts to the mean, silver could reach a price of $80 per ounce based on the historical 15:1 ratio. While I encourage being cautious in your estimates, such gains are not out of the question when considering the current cost of mining silver as a primary metal.

Never again would gold be more valuable than silver. There are once-in-a-lifetime opportunities. I recommend beginning to accumulate as much silver as your current situation would allow. I recommend placing circulated silver dollars in your physical possession. Since there is no dealer reporting provisions for circulated silver dollars, they can be purchased and sold privately. They are easily identifiable by almost any American, and they include a substantial amount of silver in a cost-effective, liquid, and portable form.

Industry can continue to use and need ever-increasing quantities of silver. With the current economic condition and the printing of money out of thin air, silver will only go up.

8 Factors which influence silver prices

One of the reasons silver is so important is the supply and demand equation: supply is small, but demand is constant. However, any perceived or real increase or decrease in supply or demand can drive rates, sometimes in ways that are disproportionate to the shift itself. For example, if a strike disrupts mining at a major producer, silver prices can spike in the short term. Similarly, news of a new application for silver, such as solar panels, will stimulate purchasing and place upward price pressure on the product.

Light-Sensitive Properties of Silver
Because of its light-sensitive properties, photography used a lot of silver at one time. There is less interest now that non-silver photography has dominated the field. Similarly, a massive stockpile of photographic film was recycled for its silver content.

Another way this factor plays out is that as prices rise, more existing silver jewelry, coins, and other items will be sold and melted down, raising the supply of silver on the market. According to Silver Institute reports, many of the readily available stockpiles of silver and scrap have been depleted at today's silver prices.

Silver prices are directly and indirectly influenced by current and emerging developments, just as they are by film technology changes. Many of these modern silver applications take advantage of physical properties unique to silver, making it nearly unreplaceable.

Contrary to popular belief, modern technology helps replace silver in more mundane applications. New types of aluminum alloys, for example, are suitable substitutes for certain low-cost mirrors. Stainless steel flatware, rather than traditional silver flatware, is increasingly common in many households.

New demand from solar photovoltaic systems and many other green applications is generally a net bullish driver for silver demand and prices.

People mostly spend a lot of money on jewelry and objects that include precious metals, such as silver, when good. Similarly, as incomes stagnate or fall, such transactions are often the first to be postponed. The growth rate and economic health in emerging markets are closely monitored as a leading indicator of demand in this segment.

Even in tough economic times, however, there is also a market for luxury goods such as watches and fine jewelry. Reports on high-end demand patterns are often used as indicators of broader economic trends, which affect silver prices.

Along with gold, silver is known as a haven investment. Silver is thought to maintain its value and buying power better than paper money and other commodities when there is economic uncertainty. As and if those economic issues turn into full-fledged crises, silver, and other precious metals prices are likely to rise dramatically.

Silver's Demand
On the other hand, a strong and vibrant economy could reduce demand for silver among investors and other buyers. While the active economy will increase demand for silver in industrial and jewelry applications, it will not produce dividends or interest income.

The impact of inflation on portfolio value is well understood by most analysts, economists, and investors. Also, nominal inflation spread over long periods falls into this category. On the other hand, silver has long been regarded as a good inflation hedge. Paper currency's value can erode due to inflation, and silver will shield you from such declines in purchasing power.

As the world's most important currency, the U.S. dollar has an inverse relationship with the price of silver. According to silver market participants, a strong dollar has historically placed downward pressure on the price of silver. At the same time, many savvy investors have an eye out for periods when the dollar is high to average down their assets by buying at a discount.

Although the gold-silver ratio's true meaning is hotly debated, there is a long-standing historical relationship between gold and silver prices. In general, if the price of gold increases or falls, so will the price of silver. Some specialists trade depending on the GSR, buying or selling as silver becomes more costly or less expensive in contrast to gold.

The level of interest rates, as stated briefly above, is an indicator of overall market conditions. Since silver investments are not made for immediate profit, some investors will choose interest payments over long-term appreciation of their silver holdings. As a result, the market price of silver is typically inversely proportional to the level of interest rates, like the dollar's strength.

Government Influence on Silver Markets

Silver markets are also affected by government decisions and policies due to their long history as a medium of trade. Though gold receives the most coverage as a reserve, central banks worldwide buy and sell silver bullion. Local mints, such as the United States Mint, use many of the world's silver supply to produce both bullion and numismatic-quality coinage.

Along with these considerations, you should be aware of the distinctions between speculation and saving, as well as the differences between short-term and long-term investing. By their very nature, marketers respond quickly to short-term factors like those listed above. These rapid changes are essential to speculators and end consumers, such as jewelry manufacturers.

On the other hand, most long-term investors are more concerned with analyzing the patterns that these variables suggest. The trick to taking a long-term view of silver investing is to take advantage of the insurance it provides, take advantage of bargains as they arise, and rest assured that the value of silver holdings will rise significantly in the years ahead.

Silver as an Investment

Silver, like other precious metals, can be used as an investment. It has been used as a source of money and a store of value for over 4,000 years, though it lost its legal tender status in developing countries when the silver standard was abolished in 1935. However, some countries mint bullion and collector coins with nominal face values, such as the American Silver Eagle. In 2009, industrial applications (40 percent), jewelry, bullion coins, and exchange-traded goods were the most common uses for silver. The world's silver reserves were 530,000 tons in 2011.

Stackers are silver and other precious metals collectors who collect for the purpose of investment (either as their primary motive or as one of several). Their collections are referred to as stacks. Collectors have different explanations for stacking silver.

Just like other commodities, the price of silver is determined by speculation and supply and demand. Because of the smaller and lower market liquidity and demand variations between the industrial and store of value uses, the price of silver is notoriously volatile as compared to gold. This can lead to a wide range of stock valuations, resulting in uncertainty.

Because of the demand for a store of value, the price of silver mostly tracks the price of gold, though the ratio may differ. The crustal silver-to-gold ratio is 17.5:1. Traders, investors, and consumers often examine the gold/silver price ratio. The price ratio in Roman times was 12 (or 12.5) to 1. The gold/silver price ratio in the United States was set by statute in 1792 at 15:1, implying that one troy ounce of gold was worth 15 troy ounces of silver; in France, a ratio of 15.5:1 was adopted in 1803. During the twentieth century, however, the average gold/silver price ratio was 47:1.

Physical Bullion
When buying physical bullion in the form of coins or bars from a dealer, you can pay a premium of 20% or more. For most of 2015 and early 2016, silver bullion bars were available for purchase at a premium of less than 7% over the spot price, although government-minted coins continue to command a much higher premium.

Physical coins have a higher premium than digital coins. For example, official distributors purchase one troy ounce (oz) American Silver Eagle Coins from the U.S. mint at a $2 premium over the fluctuating silver spot price and then sell them for a premium of $3.50 to $5.50 oz over silver spot prices, depending on market conditions.

Every year, millions of Canadian Silver Maple Leaf and American Silver Eagle coins are bought as investments. The Canadian Silver Maple Leaf has a face value of CA$5, the American Silver Eagle's face value is US$1, the Britannia has a face value of between £0.20p and £10, and there are several other silver coins with higher legal tender values, such as CA$20 silver coins. Although these bullion coins are legal tender, they are rarely recognized by shops and are rarely seen in circulation, in comparison to pre-debasement 'junk' or 'constitutional' silver coins, which are still seen in circulation on occasion.

Since September 2005, the silver's price has risen steadily, starting at around $7 per troy ounce and eventually hitting $14 per troy ounce for the first time in late April 2006. In April 2006, the monthly average price of silver was $12.61 per troy ounce, and on November 6, 2007, the spot price was about $15.78 per troy ounce. It was hovering around $20 per troy ounce in March 2008. However, due to the impact of the credit crisis, the price of silver fell by 58 percent in October 2008, along with the price of other metals and commodities. Due to monetary inflation and increased concerns about the solvency of governments in the developed world, especially in the Eurozone, silver had rebounded to a 31-year high of $49.21 per ounce on April 29, 2011.

9 Should i buy silver?

Silver is real money. Silver is not part of our current currency, but the facts are it is still money. Silver and Gold are the real true forms of money and the reason is because it is not printed fiat currency which goes down in value every day. When I say real money, I mean physical assets like Silver and Gold, not contracts or certificates. These paper investments do not have the same benefits that real assets do.

If you hold real assets in Silver, then you do not need anyone to keep their word or contract while with other investments you do.

There is no default risk when you hold real assets in Silver. You can not say that with other investments. In fact, Silver has served as real money for thousands of years.

Silver is cheap. This serves to protect you against any crisis, unlike Gold. Silver is much more affordable to average investors and it will help you maintain a standard of living. In fact let us say you want to send someone a gift of $1,000 dollars or more and you can not afford that. You can send them a real hard asset like Silver instead which is always going up in value.

Silver is not only cheaper to buy, but also more practical when you want to sell it. You can sell as much or as little Silver you want or need at any time.

Silver is in high demand globally. The demand for Silver is growing and all the major government mints have been experiencing record number of sales. You can see this easily in China and India. They have long histories towards precious metals including Silver.

10 How to buy silver easily

Silver can be purchased in many ways, but I need to caution you about scammers. During the last 12 months there has been a tremendous increase in fake Silver coins, bars and slabs. The same is true for all precious metals so I no longer risk buying Silver on eBay. There are some reputable online coin companies, and you are reasonable safe buying from them. The biggest problems we see are long delays to receive you Silver. I cannot speak for you but when purchasing Silver, I do not want to wait three or four weeks for delivery.

In addition to where to buy, you should consider how easy it is. It should be easy enough to setup a regular purchase frequency. The best plan includes regular increases in your Silver holding. An increasing concern as inflation is rapidly increasing.

Along with where to buy, and how often, consider price. You want a dealer who is consistent and fair with premiums. Premiums are the cost over and above the listed "spot" price. You can think of premiums like taxes when you buy other items. You see the price on the shelf and understand the total at the register will be higher. Premiums have been increasing with demand, but many dealers are price gouging.

After months of evaluation, I have found a Silver buying club that has been in business many years, has Silver in stock at very fair prices, packages all shipments under video surveillance and ships very fast. I typically receive my Silver in about five days after order. I call this Silver for the Win! You can learn more at www.SilverForTheWin.com

Pure Silver bullion coins from all around the word
Truly stunning assets mad of 1oz pure 999+ fine Silver
Automatically receive coins monthly with Auto-Wealth Plans
Ability to adjust coin quantity received monthly anytime

11 Closing

Silver belongs to a select category of valuable commodities that includes gold, platinum, and palladium since it is known as a "precious metal." Because of its special characteristics and relative scarcity, this lovely white metal has always been in high demand. Although demand for silver has remained consistent, prices have been volatile. The following are ten factors that influence silver price fluctuations.

Understanding silver price patterns necessitates a detailed review of a range of variables. These market dynamics operate against one another, making silver price analysis more challenging. When production prices hit a certain amount, any commodity price below that level means less mining and supply. On the other hand, higher silver prices encourage more expensive mining and processing, increasing supply. Therefore, silver is very important. It is actual money and way better than paper money.

Buying and holding Silver is just what you need as we accelerate into this new economy. Fiat currency, that is paper currency with nothing to give it value is flooding every country on earth. The US is no different. We have never seen anything to this extent and as the buying power of our fiat currency goes down it may very well be those with hard assets like Silver can survive through until things get better.

I asked many people why they buy Silver and here are some of their reasons:

Use it to store some excess cash for retirement age

Silver is shiny

A hobby, the thrill of getting a piece

The hunt! Trying to get something for a good price

To leave the kids something that is going to be worth something

Started two months ago and it stops me from spending cash savings

I was looking for a hobby that would not destroy my wallet

Doomsday and its awesome having an international hard currency

Something to give my kids one day

I like it. Also, something to spend my money on that is not a complete waste

It was a one-time purchase that kept growing

My savings account was only getting about $4 a month in interest

It is an emotional control. I put a couple rounds in my pocket and make less emotional purchases like coffee and soda etc.

This has helped me greatly to buy more assets

I am worried about the next economic crash and a bail out to save the banks

I like to spend. I have a hard time saving money but over the last five years I have saved over 2,000 ounces. It is my emergency fund

Buying silver helps protect me from inflation

I buy silver with the money from yard sales. I cannot lose

Our government is greedy and prints money non-stop. I must buy silver to sleep at night

It is better than spending money on alcohol

I think the economy is going to crash and it will help me get through the worst of it

Hedge against inflation

It is cheaper than gold and a bargain to buy

I buy silver for my daughter so when she is grown up she will have a head start

I buy silver and enjoy giving silver dollars to my grandchildren on birthdays

It is like playing the lottery except I win now and will win bigger in the future

I hope you have enjoyed this book and it has given you some useful information. I encourage you to take action to protect your financial future. If that leads you to buy Silver join us online and in our Facebook Group.

You can get learn more at www.SilverForTheWin.com

ABOUT THE AUTHOR

John Michael Weir has been an avid collector of coins for many years. More recently John has researched economic news, especially the effects of inflation over the last 100 years. The evidence is clear that hard assets like silver are the best investments in 2021. After testing different options for purchasing silver John selected Quick Silver as his primary source because of low premiums, great selection and fast shipping.